ALBERTO PINTO

Moderns

ALBERTO PINTO
Moderns

RIZZOLI
NEW YORK

First published in the United States of America in 2002 by
Rizzoli International Publications, Inc.
300 Park Avenue South, New York, NY 10010
www.rizzoliusa.com

ISBN-13: 978-0-8478-2465-6
ISBN-10: 0-8478-2465-9
LCCN: 2002090783

Designed by Alain Pouyer

Cover: A swimming pool in São Paolo.
Page two: Sitting corner in Alberto's Pinto agency.
Page 8: Marbella, a bedroom in the nanner of Joan Miró.
Page 10: São Paulo, a dining room in the Art Deco Style.
Back cover: Entrance hall of an office building in Paris.

Printed and bound in China

2006 2007 2008 / 10 9 8 7 6 5 4 3

CONTENTS

We would like to thank the following people
for their assistance:

Nicole Fallot, project coordinator;
Marianne Robic and Fleurs d'Alma
for floral arrangements.

Many thanks also to the design staff
for their warm welcome and suggestions.

P.R.
W.W.

When Alberto Pinto comes to mind, he is usually classified, and quite naturally so, as one of the decorators who has the gift of bringing back the great moments of the past to fashion. Indeed, he is unequaled in his love and understanding of expressing the grandiose and the magnificent through the decorative styles of the eighteenth and nineteenth centuries. He is a brillant matchmaker of objects, organizing wildly improbable or poetically touching marriages. Quite surprisingly however, his cult of the past was late in coming. His first decorating inclination was decidedly modern. Before designing, he exercised his eye while photographing the decors imagined by others for magazines during the Sixties. It was natural that one day he would try his hand at decorating. Lucite, painted rattan and glowing neon were favorites and not a thought for more traditional materials. Alberto was a man of his times: simplicity, functionality, even frillless minimaiism, expressed with strict, forceful lines. Spaces bathed in colorful fluorescent light with kinetic paintings on the walls.

Although the chain of commissions would eventually redirect his esthetic route toward grand international decoration and he would join the select club of men of taste with an innate flair for combining styles and periods. Actually, Alberto Pinto is still a man of his times. His preference goes to open, inventive space conceived as a showcase for contemporary creations. The realizations presented in this book illustrate how the decorator interprets the present. In some cases he updates classic spaces, whereas in others he has collaborated with architects in decidedly contemporary volumes in the headquarters of international corporations. In these reportages there are, equally, examples of the decorator's know-how when he must outfit luxury jets or yachts. Hundreds of photographs will all have in common an Alberto Pinto in phase with the late twentieth and beginning twenty-first centuries.

From his native Morocco, the decorator has kept a generous, infectuous smile which betrays his easy-going Mediterranean charm. Childhood memories are happy, calm and remarkably uneventful in the midst of a loving family. In matters of taste, all eyes were turned toward Paris, which exerted a great influence on his hometown, post-colonial Casablanca. The young Alberto's budding tastes rapidly came to prefer the occidental "French touch" to the nearby oriental models. As time passed, when Pinto analyzed his unique decorative vocabulary, he would realize that his love of daring juxtapositions, lavish use of colors, love of comfort and sense of pomp were derivative of his oriental Maghrib. In the meantime, he amassed the quintessence of worlds of design from his travels, namely American practicality, British chic and French elegance. There was little surprise that this composite style would appeal to an international clientele whose occupations and tastes tend by their very nature toward the eclectic.

Raised in a large home, Pinto has the nostalgia of wide open spaces indoors, of almost gigantic proportions. It is in this context that his ideas are most aptly expressed.

Family traditions concerning relatives and friends often showed him as a youth in Casablanca that there was always room for one or two more at the dinner table. Entertaining was an intuitive art based on centuries of Oriental customs.

His approach tends to enlarge available space, as if he were actually capable of moving walls. This philosophy abhors the boring and the sedate. When, however, he creates intimate areas, he avoids the obvious. Bedrooms take on the comfortable airs of a drawng room; drawing rooms forget to be grandiloquent and are transformed into cozy spots ideal for quiet evenings with close friends. Without a doubt, there are no satisfactory shortcuts to sum up Pinto's decorating manner. In his own words, he considers himself as a discreet advisor of the Captains of Industry and the jet set, fashioning their daily life. "L'Homme pressé" Paul Morand's legendary character is the implicit model.

Color and warmth, he admits, are necessities. Memories of the Moroccan climate were most certainly decisive. Cold, uninviting interiors are banished from his vocabulary. Choices are intended to reassure and they do. Ancient memories surge forth as he deftly manipulates classic styles with a twist. Geographical context and the corresponding ambience are more often mixed then matched. Refusing to turn his back on his roots, Pinto nonetheless best fancies the Orient in European and especially French interiors. But immoderate taste for cross-referencing should not conceal the fact that Alberto Pinto's choices in furniture are up to date as are his sense of harmony and his handling of space. He is equally sensitive to passing revivals, of the Fifties, Seventies, etc. He is unequaled in his use of acidulent chromatic harmonies, which at first puzzle before becoming obviously appropriate. His combinations which betray his knowledge of fashion and couture place him in the fore of interior decoratators. This book is brimming with cases in point.

OFFICES IN A PARIS MANSION

Off the left side of the courtyard a majestic eighteenth stone staircase with a robust wrought iron railing coils to the top of the mansion. The different departments of the agency open on to the four levels.

A stone's throw from the quintessentially royal Place des Victoires, Alberto Pinto installed his agency in the historic seventeenth century Hôtel des Victoires near the center of the capital. He undertook its restoration with the respect he has always shown when updating such prestigious real estate. One enters the agency through the grand carriage entrance opening onto a courtyard. Offices fan out from this central axis. Leading off it, a hallway is guarded by larger-than-life armored warriors. Boxwood balls placed in generously curved silver pots where one would expect more traditional terra-cotta planters, flank the frescoes, in the taste of the eighteenth century Italian baroque. Alberto Pinto is fond of sprinkling unanticipated details like this throughout his decors.

On the second floor, overlooking the street, a sitting room flanks the sample room and documentation library. Comfortable sofas and armchairs covered with ecru linen surround a high-wool Moroccan rug executed after a cartoon by Alberto Pinto. An oversized collage by the Spanish artist Antonio Valdès faithfully reflects the vigorous character of the master of the mansion.

Above: The library occupies the left side of the sitting room. A wealth of carefully classified documents is available to the agency staff on the floor-to-ceiling oak bookcases.

In the documentation room, a Forties commode stands against a pier flanked by windows dressed with striped fabric designed by Alberto Pinto for Nobilis.

The walls are covered with tall bookcases in light-colored wood. The wicker baskets are filled with carefully classified and tagged samples arranged by color and material.

To the right of the sitting room, floor-to-ceiling bookcases line the walls around a large light-colored wooden conference table from the 1940s. Chairs with simple, white line slipcovers surround it. To the left of the sitting room, almost identical tall bookcases frame the room. The shelves are lined with wicker baskets brimming with hundreds of swatches and samples of fabric, tiles and wallpaper. These are the basic building blocks with which the agency decorators create chromatic and texture harmonies.

This space has the charm of old-fashioned supply rooms which, drawer after drawer, carton after carton, attest to the consummate know-how of French craftsmen. Alberto Pinto is acutely conscious that their talents are indispensable in translating his ideas into reality. His reputation is inextricably linked to their skill.

Above and following page: A conference room serves as the antechamber to Alberto Pinto's office. An imposing Forties work table and chairs temper the reigning classical atmosphere. The delicately curved lines of the chairs recall the carvings on the wainscoting.

Alberto Pinto's officies adjacent to a conference room with furnishings from the 1940s. Despite the existing carved wood wainscoting eighteenth century, the decorator adamantly wanted to work in surroundings with a contemporary flavor. Reminiscent of an artist's studio, large windows shaded by sheer curtains open onto the courtyard, whereas four iron-framed glass doors mark the corners of the office. Placed on a Thirties rug, a light-colored Neo-Renaissance wooden table surrounded by high-backed chairs is used for conferences. On the walls, Alberto Pinto has hung works by Christian Bérard and by his friend Yves Saint-Laurent.

Pages 24-25: Light pours through the large bays in Alberto Pinto's office, which opens onto the central courtyard. Four glass and iron doors frame the room corners.

A bronze head from the Cubist period sits atop a black lacquered chest of drawers.

An immaculate white plaster column in the pure Forties style by Pascaud is placed near the large bays shaded by billowy white curtains.

Preceding pages: The bottom of the dining room walls are covered with blue tiles; above, engraved copper plates hang in groups of three or four.

In the visitors' restroom the fresco wall decor by Florence Derive imitates the gray marble slabs on the floor. Above a small bench, two paintings complete the contemporary note of the glass and stainless steel sink.

THE BALMAIN BOUTIQUE IN PARIS

In revitalizing the look of the Pierre Balmain couture house, Alberto Pinto sought to create a poetic ambiance within a rather grand Louis XIV setting. The bronze railing is an interlacing of branches along which snails inch and monkeys run.

In designing the Balmain boutique on rue François Ier, Alberto Pinto created the perfect setting for the prestigious house of haute couture. Light-colored walls are the discreet backdrop for the omnipresent bronze stair railing where stylized birds and animals perch on entangled branches. Modernized versions of classic French Boulle furniture, black lacquer enhanced by simple gilt bronze trim, provide elegant contrasts. Bold, geometrical black-and-light striped floor marquetry of wenge and oak produces a magical effect on the entire space.

Like paintings by old Dutch masters, mirrors in wide black frames reflect the sales area dominated by the graphic floor marquetry. The latest creations are displayed in recesses on the simplest of racks. Exposed flush against the walls, the coats and frocks bring to mind works by Jim Dine. In fact, a customer might easily imagine she is browsing in an art gallery.

In strict control, Alberto Pinto played light against dark throughout: on the floor, walls, and furniture. The happy marriage of Boulle-inspired tables with gilt bronze trim on striped marquetry spans a stylistic gap of several centuries.

Display cases framed in the same black lacquered wood as the mirrors pursue the museum theme.

A veritable menagerie has taken refuge in the twisted branches of the espaliered tree railing.

Following pages: Wall and floor display cases serve as elegant foils for the Balmain creations which become abstract silhouettes or volumns sculpted by shafts of light.

Preceding pages:
Artistic rendering by agency artists of the boutique.

CORPORATE RESTAURANT

According to Alberto Pinto, in order to humanize the often impersonal reception zones in business offices, well-defined volumes and the pertinent use of sculpture lend airs of an art gallery.

Alberto Pinto welcomes the challenge offered by spaces where the grand style is largely proscribed. Here his mission was to transform a rather neutral space into a privileged, sociable area where executives and their international guests can dine in smart surroundings.

Conviviality is the key word and the interior decorator kept this in mind as he conceived the reception area. Sculptures and palm trees welcome diners before they enter the restaurant. Guests' first impressions are all important. Pinto wanted them to feel they were entering an elegant, inviting restaurant and not a family self service. The high chrome and brightly colored vinyl stools of the nearby bar, as well as the sweeping curves of the dark wood room dividers/banquettes in the main dining room, set the right tone for a fashionable eating house.

*On a table next to the bar,
an improvised still life of white-glass
water jugs await the thirsty.*

Strict order reigns in the cafeteria of the
corporate restaurant. Canary yellow stools
surrounding bass drum tables pep up the scene.

An office building

The chandeliers Alberto Pinto has designed for the lobby are inspired by a much smaller 1920s model he came across in New York.

When Alberto Pinto is commissioned to outfit an office building, he always dedicates his full attention to those sometimes overlooked communal zones - lobbies, reception areas and hallways - where workers, clients and visitors cross paths several times each day. These areas represent small but important building pieces of the corporate image, ones which can hardly be disregarded. He can choose the grandiose and breathtaking or the intimate and reassuring, among other solutions. Here in the Défense business district on the outskirts of Paris in a building designed by the architects Burstin & Burstin, Pinto's references were decidedly American Grandiose. Truncated obelisk columns, oversized tapered chandeliers and monumental sculptures all contribute to impress and reassure those who enter.

Stone, steel, bronze and dark
leather are the refined, eminently
masculine materials that Pinto
finds effective when he wants
to underscore the imposing
dimensions of spaces.
The stylized world globe is a subtle
reminder of the international
character of the business
transactions handled by the
companies. The free-standing
metal sculpture sends another
message: that company officials
are in touch with contemporary
culture and remain in direct
contact with present times.

Preceding pages:
Visible from the street, Jean Faucher's
monumental steel sculpture in
the otherwise sober lobby conveys a
message of modernity.

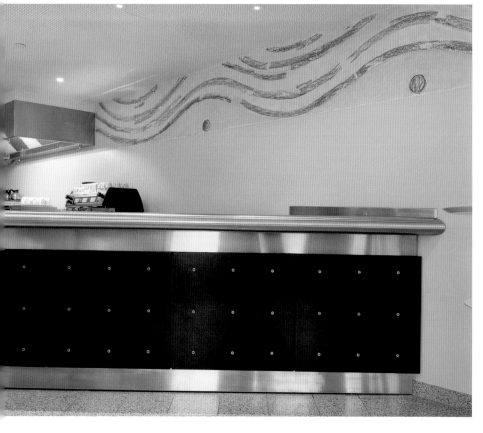

As is often the case, the cafeteria has been relegated to the basement. In order to help diners forget this, the decorator has livened the eating area with an upbeat palette of bright colors.

Following pages:
Alberto Pinto can become very playful in his treatment of often neglected corridors and service areas. A perfect case in point, this hallway has been visually lengthened by a succession of monochrome canvases carefully spaced along the wall.

A Boeing 737

Pages 62-65:
Artistic renderings of the plane interior and
one of the sitting areas.
Pages 66-67:
View of one of the sitting areas.

The sleek, aerodynamically tapered fuselage of this Boeing 737 hides an even more elegant interior of a business jet on hire to international executives. Alberto Pinto was called in to outfit it in such a manner that the time spent aboard would be as pleasurable and comfortable as possible.

The succession of rooms and sitting areas allow for a diversity of uses: they can be quiet corners for rest or reading as well as for small meetings. Traditional cabins seating twelve, more conducive to larger groups, have been arranged like spacious sitting rooms.

When designing the interior of a jet, Alberto Pinto lays out the basic spaces, relying on comfortable forms and soft, natural materials.

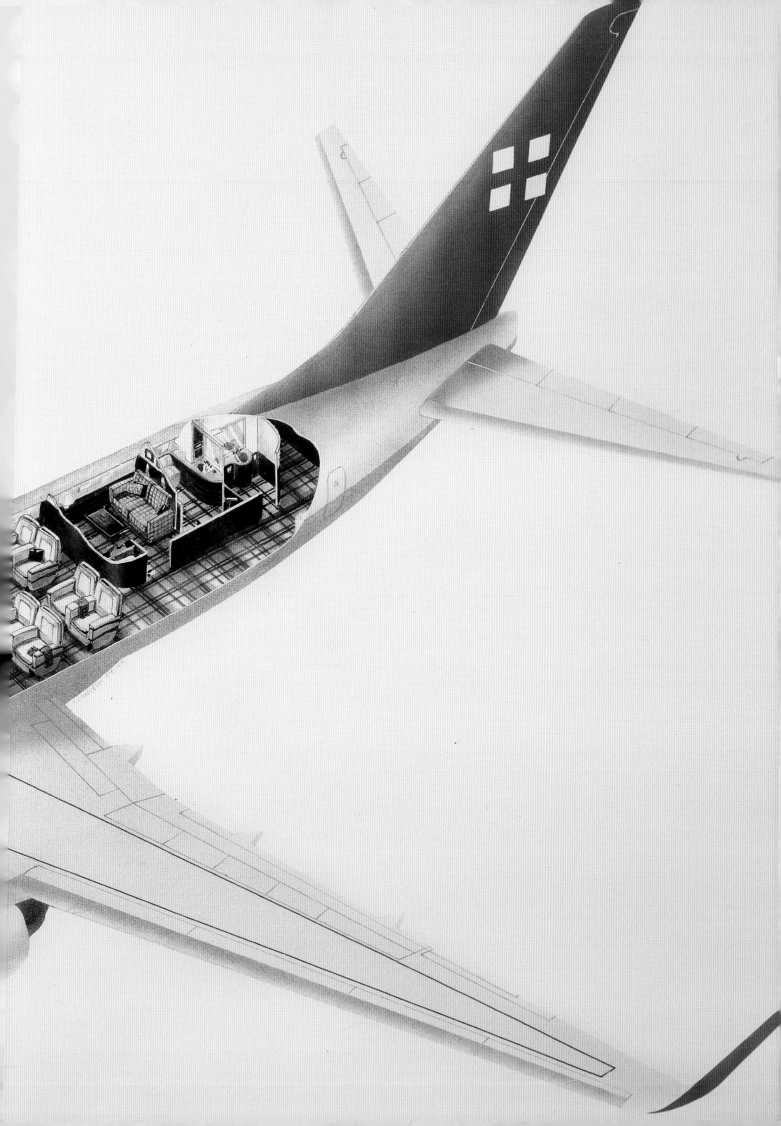

From the furniture and accessories chosen, this is an essentially masculine world: Pinto's reference was the understated appointments of luxury automobiles. Leather is king. Ebony-veneer partitions separate the cabins, and the enlarged tartan plaid carpet running the entire length of the jet unifies the interior.

Exactly as one would expect to find in a luxurious apartment, refined amenities are within reach to make flying time stressless and enjoyable.

Club Méditerranée II

A proud five-master, The Club Med II evokes the nostalgic days of long sea voyages on luxury liners. Passengers leaves worries and daily pressures on the quay and, once on board, are pampered in a world of carefree pleasure.

Alberto Pinto has collaborated with the Club Méditerrannée on numerous projects and more particularly on their two cruise liners. 187 meters in length, the Club Med II is a motor-driven yacht with accommodations for 436 passengers. Floating palaces of the past were Pinto's obvious inspiration. Throughout the vessel, from the sitting rooms to the alleyways, he has utilized an evocative palette of blues, the aquamarines of tropical lagoons and intense azures of warm South Seas, to conjure up a world of endless relaxation. The Club Med II is a haven for vacationers seeking to escape reality as they slip effortlessly back to the time of transoceanic crossings aboard legendary sailing vessels.

Throughout the ship, Alberto Pinto has utilized elements of the nautical vocabulary. Halls, corridors and staircases leading to and from decks, bars and restaurant walls are lined with traditional metal ship railings which are usually reserved for exterior alleyways. Although Pinto chose conventional nautical materials -rope, teakwood and heavy canvas- for their strength and durability, they are also very comfortable and reassuring. Painted decorations by Florence Derive are composed of easily recognizable, vigorous motifs and images inspired by modern masters.

Orange and blue coral and starfish à la Matisse encircle the columns in the main salon.

Dining rooms on ocean liners are very important places.
It was traditional for these spaces to be a demonstration of
refinement and the expert know-how of the craftsmen who
participitated in furnishing them.
Elegant yachts of the Thirties came to mind when Pinto
designed this dining room with its striped upholstery
armchairs. The same motif presented horizontally was printed on the curtain fabric. The atmosphere is relaxed and
refreshing.

*Despite the accumulation of tables
and chairs, the room inspires its diners with
tranquillity.*

Inspired by a Modern-Style model, the floor lamps are interpreted as industrial street lampposts with a solid metal protection girdling the light.

Following pages:
Artistic renderings of various lounge areas.

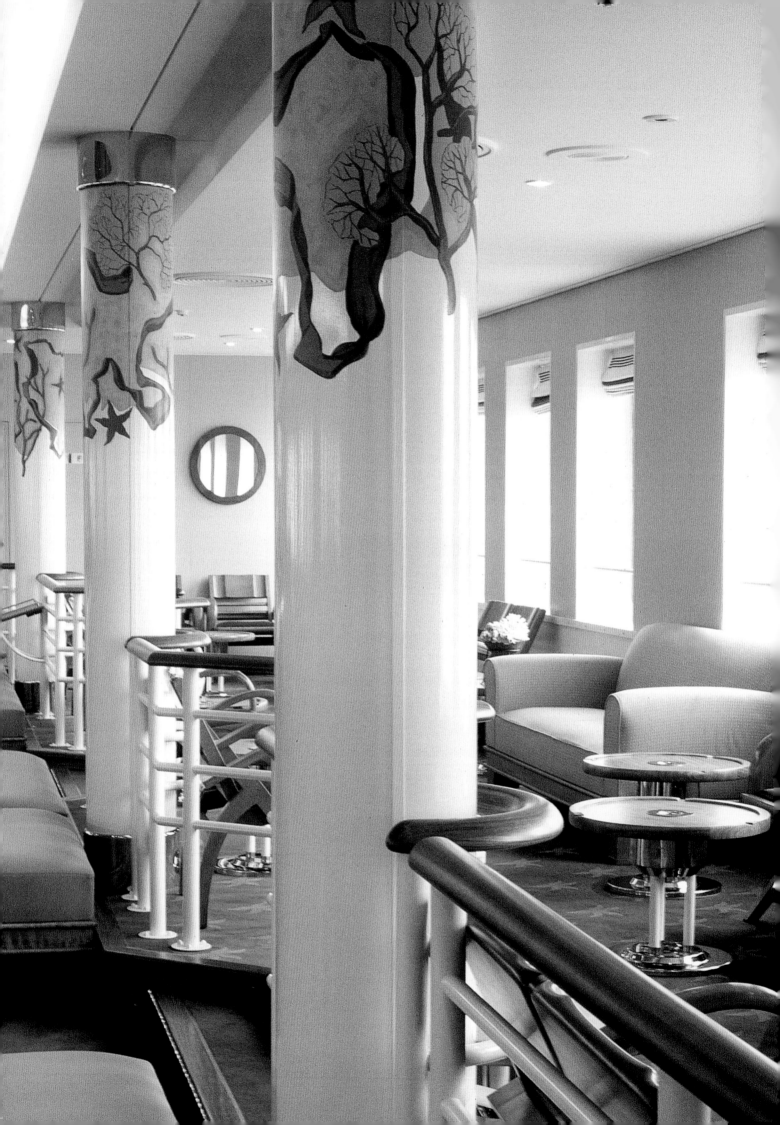

Relaxing is an important ship activity. This remained foremost in the decorator's mind as he outfitted lounges with deep sofas and wide armchairs. The marine motifs woven into the carpeting are similar to those painted on the columns and serve as the leitmotif linking the different levels of the ship.

Spacious leather armchairs with inlaid wood armrests flank a marble gueridon framed by a brass railing. On the carpeting, brightly colored starfish lie next to curious curved lines.

Passengers spend a good deal of time on the numerous decks surrounding the ship, like terraces overlooking the sea. They must be inviting, convivial spaces to sun or to doze off in the shade depending on the hour, or simply to gaze over the endless blue seas. The decorative repertoire is dominated by wood and lacquered metal.

On the promenade deck teakwood lounge chairs face the sea. Cushions of different colors syncopate the seemingly endless line of chairs.

The cabins were outfitted to give guests a feeling of intimacy and space in limited quarters. The decorator resorted to built-in furniture elements. Take, for instance, the rounded edge of the desk which is a column containing shelves, storage space and a pivoting television. The bedspread and curtains are in matching fabric, and fish-like arabesques dance on the carpet.

Preceding pages:
A view of an informal dining room with
ceramic-tiled walls and rattan and metal
chairs surrounding square tables.

VACATION HOUSE IN MARBELLA

The indoor and outdoor pool is the dramatic highlight of this quintessentially Mediterranean architecture.

I n Marbella, Spain, Alberto Pinto has designed the interior of a large vacation house where family and friends come together throughout the summer months. The architecture is forceful, with numerous windows, patios and terraces opening onto the surrounding landscape, bathing the house in Andalusian sunlight. An integral element of the whole, a spacious pool serves as the quite spectacular link, one must admit, between the interior and exterior, passing under white arches and along thick walls.

The nature theme is continued on the floors, where simple embedded-pebble friezes replace wood marquetry.

Preceding pages:
View of the outdoor dinning room.

Pinto wanted the interior of this vacation house to appear as a series of inviting open spaces. Hence, the walls have been left white, further enhancing the embedded-pebble floor decorations. Natural fabrics and materials abound, for example, benches are covered with woven reeds. Straw hats hang on the walls like proud hunting trophies.

Left and following page:
The indoor dining room is decorated in a strict, neutral manner. Twin mirrors flank a niche where a Javanese gong balances atop a teakwood column.
A mirror-like lacquered table and simple chairs with woven backs occupy the center of the room.

Pages 98-99:
The same strict style dominates the main sitting room where the decorative centerpiece is the carved wood caisson ceiling.
Pages 100-101: In the smaller sitting room Alberto Pinto deftly uses contrasting colors to create a more eclectic atmosphere. Back to back sofas are heaped with colored cushions.

The fresh colors of the murals inspired by Miró add an impertinent youthfulness to this bedroom.

The decoration of the bedrooms were opportunities for playful pastiches where Alberto Pinto could express his tastes in modern art. Here murals by Florence Derive are tributes to Joan Miró. The striking colors of the murals are repeated in the draperies, cushion covers and bedspread. In another bedroom, in order to create a warm, intimate, but unexpected decor, trompe l'œil wood paneling is used as a backdrop for Picasso engravings.

Above: Trompe l'oeil marquetry
wall paneling is the perfect foil, according
to Alberto Pinto's elegant but upbeat
approach, for three color engravings
by Pablo Picasso.
Following page:
In the adjoining bath, walls are equally
painted trompe-l'oeil.

In guest bedrooms, the decorator brings into play different repertoires. A classic arrangement of classic furnishings is transformed by a refined coquetry: large wrought-iron foliated scrolls hung on the walls.

A quiet corner for reading, with soft lighting from a pair of floor lamps and photographs of New York street scenes on the wall.

Bathrooms are another exercise in refinement for Pinto. He enjoys repeating a detail there he has used elsewhere in the house. Variations of the embedded pebble freizes cover the floors.

Following pages:
View of the kitchen and breakfast area.
The atmosphere is American Fifties.

A boat on the Mediterranean

Like a floating apartment, the boat was designed by Alberto Pinto in order to find all the comforts of a city dwelling in the middle of the Mediterranean Sea. Enormous sofas piled high with cushions, decorated wood paneling, window with curtains and draperies or blinds all contribute to the illusion of an apartment on terra firma. Only the gentle rocking reminds guests to climb to the deck to take advantage of the view. Pinto's deft handling of the subtle contradition between the interior and the exterior is typical of his art of transposition. The results are doubly rewarding, a relaxing cruise on the appeasing Mediterranean.

Meals are taken on the scored teakwood deck on cushion-covered stools around matching tables.

Delicate tints of vanilla and egg shell dominate in the sitting and dining rooms where highly polished lacquered walls and ceilings enlarge the space. On a panther rug the scene appears even more urban, with refined details on the furnishings, as in the studding on the armchairs and the carved wood friezes edging the coffee tables.

The only hint of the marine setting is the rope appliqués on cushions.

Directly inspired by the 1940s, the armchairs with straw-covered frames and oak furnishings belong to an esthetic vocabulary quite removed from what one would expect on a yacht. The distancing from the traditional nautical repertoire surprises guests and offers the perfect setting for jet-set weekends or discreet business gatherings.

In the dining room, deep upholstered armchairs with contrasting trim are placed around the table. A tall, sculpted wood floor lamp provides light.

Heading	194 deg
Altitude	-21 feet
True Airspeed	115 mph
Ground Speed	0 mph

A Business Jet

Alberto Pinto has remained old-fashioned in thinking that traveling is a privileged moment demanding calm and comfort. Polished mahogany and handsewn leather are decorative leitmotifs.

*Following pages:
One of the sitting areas at mealtime.
Pages 122-123:
Artistic renderings of the cabin with details of the armchairs.*

Alberto Pinto is past master in the art of outfitting private jets with refined amenities. In this essentially masculine world of speed and luxury, the esthetic codes of craftsmen who produced legendary motor cars and yachts of the past continue to provide the criteria of quality. Utmost comfort is the byword and the best defense against jet lag for those who cross time zones like most others cross streets. The seats are deep-padded, enveloping leather armchairs that lull passengers to sleep or let them daydream as clouds fly by, and which swivel easily for meals or meetings. They can also be completely turned around to facilitate conversation. In another of the spaces are a traditional bedroom and an adjacent bathroom where specially designed elements defy the spatial limitations.

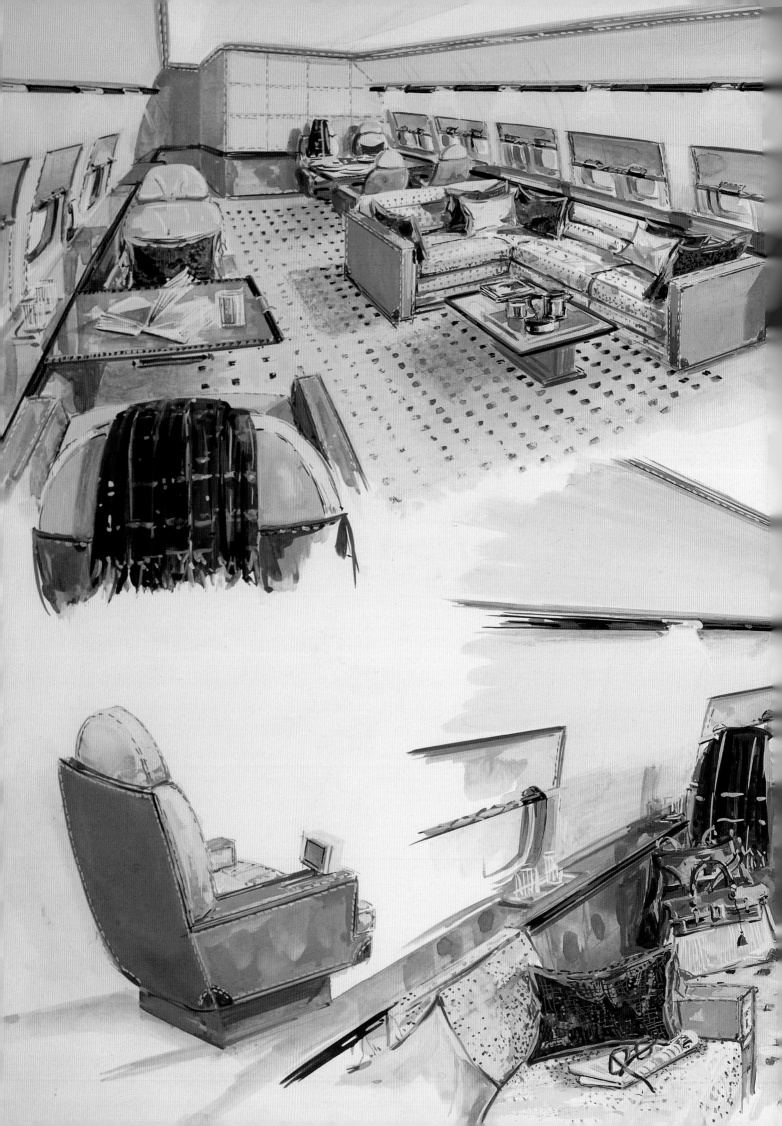

When passengers leave the public areas of the plane, they find themselves in equally tasteful settings: bath and restrooms dominated by marble, wood and glass.

Within the fuselage of this Boeing 737, Alberto Pinto has outfitted a master bedroom worthy of the best hotels. Walls are tufted with wool cloth, insulating the room from noise and the large bed is dressed with the finest linens. The bathroom is complete, and the appointments were constructed using the same noble materials as in the other areas of the jet.

Preceding pages: View of the bedroom.

IN SÃO PAULO

Preceding page: Under the lacquered surface of one of a pair of tables by Hervé Van der Straten, gilt wrought-iron figures inspired by Henri Matisse encircle the base in an intoxicating dance.

Spheres of differing circumferences alternating with fluted wrought-iron bars compose the railing of the monumental staircase that plays with Art Deco conventions to structure the apartment space.

In this gigantic residence in São Paulo, Brazil, the decorator equally carried out the prerogatives of an architect. Linking different levels in the house, the monumental staircase with bold symmetrical elements is ample proof of Alberto Pinto's capability in this dual role. A work of pure bravura, the structure with its metal railing supported by white spherical balusters removes all reference to scale in the entrance hall and guests are greeted by somewhat overwhelming grandiloquence. Sitting atop oversized tables, a pair of tall vases reminiscent of Ruhlman flank the staircase in a clear tribute to the Twenties Art Deco style.

Left: Close-up on the materials utilized in the main sitting room: lustrous silks and velvets coalesce with sparkling crystal and bronze.

Preceding pages:
On the upper level, the rectilinear lines of the railing and the Constructivist design of matching rugs are reflected in the sliding glass doors of the dining room.

Following page:
The staircase dominates the main salon, which is divided into separate siiting areas. In the foreground, the laquered wood grouping is in the Art Deco style, while generous sofas and comfortable armchairs covered in panther form another conversation corner.

Preceding page:
A black-laquered boudoir grand piano is the center of attention in the small music room. Paintings by Clovis Graciano and sculptures of jazz musicians complete the scene.

With the velvet panther armchairs, the grand salon seems to be a Hollywood film set. The overall effect is further heightened by wide bay windows affording a panoramic view of São Paulo, like a wraparound mint-blue movie screen reflecting evenings, the ever-changing image of the city lights and the starlit sky.

Following pages:
The grand salon with its panoramic view of São Paulo is illuminated by a gigantic glit-metal chandelier.

A recumbent marble figure sits on the glass coffee table, while two bronze figures by Stockinger guard the sliding doors opening onto the entrance hall.
The atmosphere is more relaxed in the gold and purple television room. The diamond-shaped Harlequin fabric of the sofa covers and curtains are in phase with the Tribute to the Circus canvas on the wall.

Preceding pages:
The gold and purple television room.

Following pages:
On the upper level, mirror-covered doors
separate the hall to the dining room.

Placed against the stucco wall panel, a female figure strikes a pose atop a deeply gadrooned pedestal with corner shell decorations.

Upon opening the mirror-covered doors, one discovers a precious wall decoration in carved stucco, a white pristine Garden of Eden full of tropical trees, fruit and ferns. Ruhlman chairs upholstered with a floral-patterned fabric surround an oval table. Several dozen red roses in as many vases and bottles are placed almost randomly on its mirror-like surface.

The mistress bedroom recalls the luxury of
the 1940s. These are a mirror-covered
cabinets, a carved giltwood headboard like
an ornate Louis XIV frame, lustrous satin
bedcovers, cushions and pillows, raw silk
draperies; all the elements come together
to create a sumptuous decor. The painting
on the wall is by Anita Malfatti .

Preceding pages:
With a pair of torchères flanking the
dressing table, the bathroom adjacent to
the mistress's bedroom was directly inspired
by the one Rateau designed
for Jeanne Lanvin.

Fresco naiads by Florence Derive take a pose on either side of the entrance to the master dressing room. Clothes are organized in a row of glass Empire-style cases.

Preceding pages:
A view of Madame's dressing room complete with a daybed in the center. Mirrors reflect carefully organized closets illuminated by Venetian ceiling lamps of painted silk by Mariano Fortuny..

For a child's bedroom Alberto Pinto uses contrasting tones of black, beige and yellow to create a rather austere setting around a group of Biedermeyer furniture. Diamond shapes and stripes are the dominant graphic patterns. The adjacent bathroom in the Neo-Classical style completes the ensemble.

Following pages:
An eight-leaf folding screen with a design inspired by Joan Miró articulates the decoration of this guest bedroom. The furnishings features distinctive details: a Frank Lloyd Wright armchair with hand-stitched wool cloth upholstery, a headboard and cushions covered by linen with mother of pearl buttons.

The study has all the comforts of a sitting room. A wall has been outfitted with open shelves for books and objects separated by closed storage areas. More than just a room to handle daily business, Alberto Pinto wanted the study to be a personal retreat. Next to the desk, deep armchairs sit on a thick pile rug. Above, a painting by Emiliano Cavalcanti hangs on the wall.

Pages 162-163:
An artist's rendering of the pool.
Pages 164-165:
The finished project.

Wrought-iron chandeliers hang above high-backed sofas covered in white linen, where swimmers can catch their breath between laps.

The spectacular pool seems straight from the pages of Utopian architects like Ledoux. The long, narrow basin edged by a wide stone curb runs along a wall marked by a series of bull's-eye windows fitted with convex mirrors. Across from the pool, a wooden terrace evoking a boat deck welcomes guests. Sunlight pours in through wide bays; tall, luminous cloth columns light the area in the evening.

Following pages:
The main entrance of the house with repoussé oxidized metal doors flanked by elaborate wall lights by Herve Van der Straeten.

VACATION HIDEAWAY IN GREECE

Preceding page:
In the entrance, the sinuous staircase
railing wraps around a generous sphere.

The sun adds a vacation feel to houses. Under its generous warmth, rooms and objects come alive. Conscious of
this invaluable natural advantage, Alberto Pinto showed
great restraint and humility in his transformation of a ven-
erable family residence into a vacation house.
Preference was given to natural materials and color contrasts abound, enhancing volumes utilizing to the fullest
the endowments of natural light.

Following pages:
In the main sitting room, brick patterns
radiate from a convex mirror over the
fireplace. White walls are decorated with
striated scoring.

In a subdued atmosphere volumes and materials take on added importance. Highly colored geometric forms and a open sphere chandelier by Dominique Bernard hanging over the oval dining table attract attention to the ceiling. Inspired by lighting sculptures by Diego Giacometti, the painted plaster circles intertwine around candle sconces. A lacing pattern in the 1940s style covers the backs of the dining room chairs

Preceding pages:
Pale green sofas with contrasting patchwork cushions line the sitting room walls. Dark wood features on seating furniture complete the setting as do the strict lines of tables, floor lamps and vases.

A low trompe-l'oeil cabinet surmounted by a pair of characteristic Forties lamps under the electric blues, golds and reds of a Fassianos.

Eclectic associations in one of the bedrooms: plaids and iron arabesques under the watchful eye of Greek shepherds by Del Re.

Alberto Pinto has taken liberties with the wall treatments. Downstairs, scored parallel lines mark the walls. Upstairs in one of the bedrooms, whitewashed walls are inlaid with pebbles in a diamond pattern like an infinitely enlarged fish net. Besides being amusing for occupants, this poetic approach allows the possibility of varying decoration with almost never ending diversity using only the simplest materials.

Herve Van der Straeten has designed bronze branches as drapery tiebacks.

Wood serves to add warmth to this bedroom dominated by fabric. Simple sandblasted and waxed boards are used as paneling behind the bed. Lacing adds points of interest.

The deforming curved surface of a convex mirror in a frame by Herve Van der Straeten provides an encapsulated view of the entire room.

AN APARTMENT IN PARIS

One enters the apartment through striking Art Deco wrought-iron double doors leading to the sitting room. The original nineteenth century moldings and stuccowork have been conserved.

For an inquisitive collector of the rare and curious with a taste for intriguing associations. Alberto Pinto has transformed a Parisian apartment of nineteenth century Haussmanian architecture and Art Deco features. Characteristic forceful ironwork dominates the foyer: symmetric panels display bouquets in vases surrounded by Greek-inspired designs on the double leaves of the majestic 1930s door.

A rotunda off the sitting room serves as the study; the existing wainscoting has been painted white. A large, dark Art Deco wood desk dominates the area, with matching tables and lamps flanking the sofa. Identically framed vintage photographs have been hung symmetrically in the recesses of the wainscoting. The blood-red resin chair by Rancillac dating from the 1970s is proof of the collector's taste for provocation.

A detail of the day bed upholstered with an embroidered and appliquéd geometric fabric.

A large arch separates the sitting room from the study. A fresco by Florence Derive lends ornateness to the rotunda ceiling over the distinctively red chair by Rancillac.

Preceding page: The sitting room ceiling is decorated with a contemporary abstract fresco in deep red tones against white clouds which reflect in the large convex mirror hanging over a Forties stone console.

Right: In the study, two bronze statuettes by Depreaux stand face to face on the coffee table.

Following pages: The white wainscoting of the main sitting room is the perfect backdrop for contrasting color schemes. Two upholstered sofas and matching leather armchairs in the Louis XIII style by Adnet stand around the fireplace on a pile carpet. A delicate Murano glass chandelier decorated with floral motifs hangs at the center of the ceiling.

A canvas by Florence Derive hangs on a wall decorated with stenciled patterns in the classic style.

Following page: Adjacent to the main sitting room in a smaller, more intimate salon stands a baby elephant from the Paris taxidermist Deyrolle. The drapery fabric by Prelle was designed after a cartoon by Ruhlman.

Another large round room with a monumental cornice framing the domed ceiling serves as the dining room. Two shelves lined with photographs, scientific objects and primitive statues follow the curve of the walls. A bronze chandelier in the Art Deco style completes the masculine setting.

A view of the enfilade from the dining room through the two sitting rooms.

Following page: In the dining room comfortable armchairs surround a metal and wood table. Photographs by Henri Foucaut line a wall shelf.

Pages 198-199:
The kitchen is organized and functional with a gay, multicolored tile floor.

An apartment on the Quai d'Orsay

In the entrance hall, the contrast of white and orange enhances the classic floor lamps by Serge Roche and the Italian crystal chandeliers.

Alberto Pinto's challenge in this project was to breathe new life into a charming, large Parisian apartment with a classic layout in order to house a precious hodgepodge of Chinese lacquer, French furniture of the Forties and objets d'art in rock crystal. From this unlikely marriage of styles was born a showcase for a collection of rare paintings.

The tall windows of the grand salon in the center of the apartment open onto the quai d'Orsay. In the very special light reflecting off the waters of the nearby Seine, objects and furniture acquire a tangible force magically transforming improbable associations.

The proportions of the grand salon are such that the decorator did not hesitate to divide it in two with a massive Coromandel folding screen, not unlike those in Coco Chanel's suite at the Ritz.

Armchairs covered in pale blue satin in the decorator's beloved Forties style surround a small jewel-like table covered with mirrors by Serge Roche. Nearby, a large canvas by Atlan hangs over the marble fireplace in front of which Pinto placed a Chinese games table and Louis XVI armchairs. Art is the center of attention: a painting by Matta hangs overs a long console lined with Asiatic antiquities and an improvised lamp, an oddly shaped obelisk of rock crystal lighted from the base.

The regal silhouette of a Velasquez duegna, a sculpture by Manolo Valdès, is in harmony with the refined atmosphere of the grand salon.

A connoisseur of modern art, Alberto Pinto playfully pairs the surrealist faces of a Victor Brauner canvas with an African mask.

On the dining room walls unfold episodes from the con-
quest of Turkey in dominant browns and ochers. This provides an excellent backdrop for a mirror-covered dining
table with scroll feet which reflects the grouping of rock
crystal spheres the decorator has grouped as centerpiece.
The same warm palette of colors is repeated on the room-size
iznik-patterned rug as well as throughout the furnishings.

*Ornate caned-backed English chairs frame
the tumultous events transpiring on the
wall panorama.*

Years of experience have developed in Alberto Pinto a decided taste for challenges, challenges which test his creative talents as well as the limits of the craftsmanship of faithful collaborators. Bedroom walls are covered with quilted, top-stiched relief patterns in the Art Deco style, protecting the occupant from outside noise. Silence is the preferred night music in this very Proustian cocoon.

Orange Murano glass lamps surround an eighth century Indian sculpture reflected in a tall mirror by Jean Royère.

The bathroom next to the master bedroom is a complex game of mirrors covering the walls. This room ceases to be only functional and becomes a cabinet of curiosities.

Following pages: The decorator's model for the kitchen was American mansions during the 1950s where spaciousness and functionality are bywords.

The adjacent master bathroom is a chamber of illusions. The decorator has reconstituted a veritable stage setting of engraved mirrors from the Forties consisting of countless curved elements creating a trellis effect. Behind these doors, Pinto has outfitted a complete jade-green dressing room. Its bright color adds a provocative splash as it is infinitely reflected throughout the bathroom. He is especially fond of creating this sort of esthethic detail which metamorphoses the space into a sitting room such that its true, rather mundane function is quickly forgotten. The pastel shades of the rug complete the intricate game of reflections.

"La Residencia" in the Canary Islands

Curved banana fronds throw dark shadows on sparkling white walls in the intense island sunlight.

Located on the Canary Islands off the northwest African mainland , "La Residencia" is a luxury vacation hotel. Alberto Pinto was commissioned for the interior design. He imagined a refined compound of modernity and tradition. The interior is punctuated with references to modern art presented in reassuring classic settings in the hacienda style. The result is an alchemy of memories and colors.

The rippling pool surface reflects a fresco drawn on the surrounding walls in an obvious tribute to the great Catalan abstract and surrealist artist Joan Miró. Above, reed screens, cacti and palms complement this multicolored hommage. Vacationers forget the quotidian in this coloring-book world.

The swimming pool is enclosed in mural-covered walls, protecting bathers from crosswinds.

Following pages:
View of the tile-covered bar. The lines of the comfortable wood and leather stools repeat those of the chairs in the adjacent dining room.

Pages 220-223:
Artistic renderings of the lounge and dining room.

Visitors arriving from the hot sun must be slightly disoriented when greeted by these typically English sitting rooms filled with comfortable armchairs and bracing colors.

The hotel interior was designed with comfortable colonial mansions in mind. The first decorative flourishes are disarmingly simple: vigorous colors -glowing blue and yellow- contrast with elegantly designed dark wood and wrought iron. Pinto complicates things by adding painted ornamentation and marquetry to already elaborate furniture inspired by Flemish and Iberian decorative styles.

Portuguese marquetry armoires, Chinese pots atop wood consoles: European decorative codes are spiced with a zesty twist of South American flair.

A Portuguese spirit reigns in the bedroom with a single row of azulejos tiles running around the walls. Bedsteads are of turned and carved dark wood. The chromatic theme of blue and yellow with the addition of white is continued in the bathrooms, constituting a pertinent résumé of the Pinto style.

In the bathroom traditional blue azulejos tiles have been colored sunny yellow.

"La Mamounia" in Marrakech

As wide as city streets, hallways at "La Mamounia" are bedecked in the traditional colors of the Maghrib. Wood paneled ceilings and pile carpeting with traditional motifs are lighted by suspened repoussé copper bowls.

Some projects are especially dear to the heart. Alberto Pinto was commissioned to review the interior of the internationally prestigious "La Mamounia" Hotel in Marrakech. He approached it with all the more affectionate respect that the hotel is a legendary institution in his native Morocco. Hallways were an excellent showcase for the outstanding workmanship of local artists and craftsmen for example, a painted coffered ceiling supported by shaped corbels in the Moresque style.

Designed by the decorator for "La Mamounia", the painted furniture patterns and the cartoons for rugs and carpets were inspired by the millennium-old traditional motifs of eternal Morocco. The geometrical rug is characteristic: woven in red, ecru and yellow wools, it is a speciality of the dyers of the royal city of Fez.

In one of the bedrooms decorated by Alberto Pinto, ornate painted doors as well as the woven diamond-patterned pile carpet are tributes to Moroccan know-how. "La Mamounia" has been at the fore of the international luxury hotel industry since its establishment in the 1930s and the criteria of comfort are especially exacting.

Preceding pages:
View of a spacious bedroom with
enveloping armchairs sitting on a colorful
carpet. A tall canvas dominates the wall
over the beds.

In a vast double room, local color is tempered by furniture in the Art Deco style, notably a pair of low, upholstered curved armchairs with wood trim, round coffee table and picture frames. These features evoke the colonial period and the Villa Majorelle in Marrakech. The arabesque designs and painted decorations covering the arched door frame, however, represent Moresque style. Oriental flavor is heightened by the large female figure in the canvas hanging over the beds.

With typical Moroccan hospitality
tantalizing local pastries and thirst-
quenching mint tea greet guests on a
1930s table.

A HOTEL IN GSTAAD

The billiards table, like the bar, avoid the anonymous character of many hotel lounge areas. Guests feels as if they are received in a warm, colorful family home.

After a day of winter sports in the snow, what a pleasure to return to the cozy atmosphere of a wood-paneled inn. This very simple idea presided over the interior design of this hotel located in Gstaad, Switzerland. Throughout, Alberto Pinto set out to interpret the basic theme of a wooden mountain chalet while adding his personal variations to create a fascinating hybrid: a large eighteenth century English manor in the Swiss mountains. Adjacent to the bar and sitting rooms, a billiards table dominates attention. Mounted antlers and a traditional paper découpage betray a mountain location.

The dining room carries guests back to the winter garden of a plush, Napoleon III hôtel particulier in nineteenth century Paris. Wood trellises lining the walls are decorated with festoons of carved flowers framing the mirror-paneled arched double doors, which enlarge the proportions of the room. This style easily evokes the luxury of grand hotels at the Belle Epoque that flourished nears spas where guests came to take the waters.

Following page: The dining room is treated like a winter garden with mirror-covered doors enlarging the space.

Wood is an all-important feature in this mountain setting. Simple, knotty planks on the walls are an unexpected modern touch.

The traditional atmosphere of mountain chalets has been preserved in the bedrooms. Wood reigns: wood paneling painted in faux bois, a naive medallion decorating the headboard and classic carved moldings in the bathroom. The latter is surprisingly formal in comparison with the simple setting of the bedroom.

A hotel in the Canary Islands

Like a drawing by David Hockney, palm trees are reflected in a mirror hanging over a neo-Seventies table.

Under the torrid sun of the Canary Islands, Alberto Pinto created the interior decoration for a hotel complex in the contemporary style, relying on pastel colors and a Sixties mood. The result is light and airy, with characteristic furnishings from the 1960s where everything seems very sculptural.

Bedrooms are generous, unencumbered spaces marked by minimalist nightstands and desks. Even the long, low cabinet is unostentatious, disappearing in the surroundings it reflects in its mirrored surfaces. Fabrics and the carpet are uncomplicated line patterns on a strict geometric surface. Throughout, paintings are systemically large abstract works, which, room after room, recount art trends of the Sixties and Seventies.

Following page:
The restrained, clear lines of this guest room have a definite California air. An almost transparent molded-wire Bertoia chair, placed against a solid-colored wall is in perfect harmony with the concentric bands of the floor lamp. A single palm frond suffices as bouquet.

Sparsely designed rooms remain simple, uncomplicated spaces leaving eccentric furniture to attract attention.
The ambiance is comfortable, bathed in the nostalgia of the Sixties. Here a lamp in pâte de verre, a vase and a free-form bowl are as much a decorative still life as a grouping of utilitarian objects.

*On lemon walls , the same color as
the mint-thin sat pads, hangs a tribute to
Sam Francis.*

Photographic credits:

Giorgio Baroni: pages 2, 8, 10, 12, 13, 14-15, 16-17, 18, 19, 20, 21, 22, 23, 24-25, 26, 27, 28-29, 30, 31, 42, 43, 44, 45, 46-47, 48, 49, 90, 91, 92-93, 94, 95, 96, 97, 98-99, 100-101, 102, 103, 104, 105, 106, 107, 108, 109, 110-111, 112, 113, 114, 115, 116, 117,130-131, 132-133, 134, 135, 136, 137, 138-139, 140-141, 142, 143, 144-145, 146, 147, 148, 149, 150-151, 152-153, 154, 155, 156, 157, 158-159, 160, 161, 164-165, 166, 167, 168-169, 170, 171, 172-173, 174-175, 176, 177, 178, 179, 180, 181, 182, 183, 184, 185, 186, 187, 188, 189, 190-191, 192-193, 194, 195, 196, 197, 198-199, 200, 201, 202-203, 204, 205, 206, 207, 208, 209, 210, 211, 212-213, 214, 215, 216, 217, 218-219, 224, 225, 226, 227, 228, 229, 230, 231, 232, 233, 234-235, 236, 237, 238, 239, 240-241, 242, 243, 244, 245, 246, 247, 248, 249, 250-251, 252, 253, 254, 255.
Roland Beaufre: 70, 71, 72, 73, 74, 75, 76, 77, 82, 83, 84, 85, 86-87, 88, 89.
Jacques Dirand: 118, 119, 120-121, 126-127, 128, 129.
Vincent Knapp (copyright Madame Figaro) 60 - 61, 66-67, 68, 69.
Mario Pignata Monti: Cover, 32 - 33 - 34 - 35 - 38 - 39 - 40-41, 50, 51, 52-53, 54, 55, 56, 57, 58-59.
Studio Harcourt: 7.
Studio Pinto: 36-37, 62-63, 64-65, 78-79, 80-81, 122-123, 124-125, 162-163, 220-221, 222-223.